Original title:
Boughs of Brilliance

Copyright © 2025 Creative Arts Management OÜ
All rights reserved.

Author: Juliana Wentworth
ISBN HARDBACK: 978-1-80567-212-8
ISBN PAPERBACK: 978-1-80567-511-2

Whispers of Luminescent Leaves

In the park, leaves giggle, sway,
They dance and poke, a cheeky display.
A squirrel wears shades, thinks he's so cool,
While the pigeons plot, like birds of a school.

Sunlight trickles, a playful tease,
The grass whispers secrets, just like the breeze.
A worm in a top hat makes quite a scene,
While ants reenact their grand magazine.

Symphony of Shimmering Canopies

Branches chat softly, in rustling tones,
As a beetle conducts, while juggling stones.
A chorus of leaves joins in with the breeze,
They're singing a tune, with scratchy old keys.

A raccoon plays drums on a hollowed-out log,
While frogs harmonize, croaking in fog.
They play all day, till the sun bids adieu,
And fireflies join in, with their glow too!

Flickering Shadows on Golden Bark

Shadows play tag on the bark so bright,
A silly old fox prances with delight.
His shadow, like him, is rather quite sly,
As it tumbles and rolls, under the sky.

A wise old owl laughs from his lofty perch,
While squirrels throw acorns in an acorn-search.
They question the shadows, where will they go?
With laughter and joy, they steal the show!

The Glow Beneath the Green

Under the leaves, there's a glimmering scene,
Where critters throw parties, so silly, so keen.
A ladybug in heels spins round, oh so fast,
While glow worms are flashing, a dance unsurpassed.

A hedgehog in glasses gives a quirky speech,
About flowers and sunshine, so dreamy to teach.
The daisies all giggle, in winds that twirl,
As the mushrooms are waltzing, in a lively swirl.

Celestial Roots and Starry Skies

In a garden full of quirks,
The carrots sport some dirty smirks.
The onions hold their breath quite tight,
While radishes dance in the moonlight.

Roses wear the silliest hats,
With daisies giggling at the spats.
The sunflowers peep, all hands on deck,
As peas start planning their next big trek.

Worms wiggle with mock flamboyance,
While clouds practice their best dance.
Frogs croak out a melody,
To cheer for roots, from A to Z.

Underneath this vibrant show,
A turtle steals the spotlight glow.
With every chuckle in the night,
The stars join in - what a sight!

The Radiant Language of Leaves

Leaves whisper secrets, oh so sly,
As squirrels in suits stroll by.
A leaf in plaid gives a cheeky wave,
While tree trunks boast their sturdy pave.

Maples wear their colors bright,
While oaks just laugh at their sheer height.
The lilacs giggle, 'What a tale!'
As breezes tease with a gentle gale.

In this forest, chatter prevails,
Where mushrooms tell of fairy tales.
The ivy hangs like it knows the way,
Turning rustles into a Broadway play.

Underneath the full moon's sprawl,
Every petal seems to call.
Oh, how nature flirts and twirls,
Bringing laughter to all the worlds!

Sunlit Saunter through Verdant Halls

On a stroll through leafy lanes,
Sunlight spills like golden grains.
Each petal prances, donning cheer,
While butterflies flutter, shifting gear.

A rabbit with a sneaky grin,
Plots to nibble on some skin.
While roses blush in vibrant hues,
As bees hum tunes of silly blues.

Under canopies, the squirrels play,
Chasing shadows throughout the day.
They tumble, trip, and softly squeak,
Their antics lighting up the week.

In this album of shades and scents,
Each moment's wrapped in raucous events.
So come along, let laughter swell,
In nature's heart, it casts its spell!

Chasing Sparks Amongst the Foliage

In dappled light where mischief creeps,
The shadows dance and the oak tree leaps.
A squirrel dons a tiny cap,
As crickets strum a crazy rap.

Fireflies waltz, with sparkles bright,
Guiding critters in the night.
A toad croaks lines that cause a grin,
While bullfrogs join the din, within.

The branches sway, with glee they shout,
While leaves twirl in a cheerful bout.
The wind laughs softly, blowing cool,
Creating wonders in this leafy pool.

As giggles echo, night unspools,
A symphony of nature pulls.
So join the chase, let spirits fly,
In the night where all things vie!

Nature's Glow: A Melodic Interlude

In the woods where squirrels dance,
Frogs leap high; they take a chance.
Leaves laugh softly in the breeze,
While flowers wear their sunny peas.

A deer with shades, so chic and spry,
Winks at birds that drift on by.
Raccoons thread through leaves like stealth,
Plotting heists for nature's wealth.

Verdant Luminosity

Caterpillars in top hats strut,
As buzzing bees form quite a nut.
Grasshoppers sing, they croon and tease,
Tickling toes with their leafy leas.

Chirping crickets throw a bash,
With fireflies glowing; oh, what a splash!
They glow like stars, yet play so shy,
In this wild party under the sky.

Gateway to the Glimmering Grove

Pixies giggle, hiding behind trees,
They trade gossip with the teasing breeze.
A turtle in spectacles reads the map,
While rabbits rehearse for their next slap.

The sun peeks in, a playful spy,
Finding worms that wiggle and cry.
Under mushrooms, the gnomes hold court,
Debating if to dance or cavort.

The Lilt of Illuminated Petals

Butterflies wear polka dot skirts,
While ladybugs share all the flirts.
The roses waltz, their perfume sweet,
And daisies hide in the grass for a feat.

A clumsy bee trips on a stem,
Losing the nectar, oh what a gem!
The garden giggles, what a scene,
Nature's humor, forever keen.

Enchantment in the Verdant Veil

In the glade where giggles sprout,
The rabbits dance and twist about.
A squirrel juggles acorns high,
While birds sing tunes that make us cry.

The flowers wear their brightest hats,
And chat with snails about the mats.
A fox in shades of sunset's hue,
Attempts a trick with a balmy dew.

A Serenade of Glowing Treasures

The glowworms twinkle in a line,
While frogs compose a silly rhyme.
They leap and croak in perfect glee,
   In hopes to join the jubilee.

The stars peek through the leafy screen,
And start a flash dance so serene.
With fireflies joining in the fun,
They sparkle brighter than the sun.

Blooming Light and Nature's Muse

A daisy dons a polka dot,
While daisies giggle at the plot.
They plot a grand parade in pink,
And share the gossip with a wink.

The bees all buzz in laughter shared,
About the winds that blow unprepared.
With petals flying here and there,
It's fashion week—without a care!

The Radiance that Lingers

The sun breaks through the leafy maze,
While critters join a sun-lit craze.
A hedgehog dons a grass-made hat,
And challenges a sleepy cat.

The butterflies take flights like dreams,
While flowers giggle in sunbeams.
With pollen fights and pollen dreams,
Nature plots its funny schemes.

Echoing Radiance of Nature's Heart

In the forest where shadows dance,
Squirrels proclaim their wild romance.
With acorns flying, they shout with glee,
Who knew trees had such jubilee?

Leaves giggle when the wind does tease,
Tickling branches with noticeable ease.
Birds hold concerts, a comedic show,
Nature's stage is the place to go.

Rabbits hop in an awkward train,
Chasing after each other's tail again.
Their bouncy antics, a silly sight,
Under the sunlight, they laugh outright.

The flowers whisper secrets so bright,
With petals fluttering, a colorful sight.
Oh, the flora knows, and so do we,
Nature's humor is the best, you'll agree!

Mellow Luster of Leaf and Sky

Leaves are playing hide and seek,
With clouds above, they giggle and squeak.
Caterpillars cruise with a stylish sway,
Pretending they're on a fun holiday.

Sunshine winks from its lofty throne,
While grasshoppers rap in a monotone.
The sky is a canvas, painted with cheer,
As butterflies weave tales, oh so dear.

Frogs croak jokes from their lily pads,
While fish splash around like giggling lads.
Together they form a lively crew,
In this green circus, there's much to do.

Nature laughs, as a gentle breeze,
Tickles the branches with such playful ease.
Life's a comedy, full of delight,
Under the mellow glow, oh what a sight!

Through the Veins of Nature's Light

Sunbeams filter through the leafy din,
Where giggling critters revel within.
A squirrel swings, trying to impress,
The woodland animals laugh, no less.

Bees buzz tunes in a quirky beat,
While ants march on with rhythm neat.
Each blade of grass joins in the cheer,
In this brilliant show, everyone's here.

The brook chuckles, splashing along,
With pebbles turning into a playful throng.
What a ballet, nature's reels of fun,
Mixing up joy, like flour in a bun.

So lift your spirits to the skies,
Join the creatures as laughter flies.
Through light and shade, a joke to find,
With nature's heart, we're all entwined!

A Revelation Among the Leaves

Peeking through the branches, oh what a view,
A chubby raccoon, looking right at you.
With a mischievous grin, it strikes a pose,
And the laughter blooms, as humor grows.

The wise old owl hoots, 'Who goes there?'
As critters gather, embracing the flare.
Even the spider spins a funny tale,
In this leafy haven, joking won't fail.

Acorns bounce like jesters on the ground,
Every creature's giggle, a blissful sound.
The trees sway gently, playing their part,
Nature's laughter sings straight to the heart.

So next time you wander through nature's embrace,
Look for the humor, in this bountiful space.
There's laughter galore in the rustle and breeze,
Among the leaves, find fun with ease!

Light's Harmony with the Earth

In the garden where mushrooms sway,
Sunflowers dance, what a display!
Pumpkins giggle, potatoes grin,
While the silly worms do the spin.

The daisies are sharing a secret tale,
While squirrels plot to swipe a kale.
A frog croaks jokes by the pond's round,
Even the fish laugh without a sound.

Bees wear hats made of pollen bright,
Buzzing tunes in pure delight.
A raindrop slips, a splash, a giggle,
As the grasshoppers join in to wiggle.

The sun, a jester, throws out beams,
Painting the sky in golden dreams.
While shadows play hide and seek,
Nature's laughter makes us cheek to cheek.

Uplifted by Nature's Glow

Under the trees where the best jokes are,
A squirrel opens a nutty bazaar.
With acorn hats and a chattering crew,
They barter for laughs, who knew?

The brook tells tales with a bubbly cheer,
Even the rocks perk up to hear.
While crickets tune up for a night-time show,
Their concert's the best, come on, let's go!

A butterfly flutters with colorful flair,
Wearing a cape and a dash of air.
While daisies giggle at the clouds above,
Who'd thought nature's quirks were full of love?

With every breeze, the giggles swell,
As the trees sway, casting their spell.
A lively chorus, nature's embrace,
In this funny realm, we find our place.

Symphony of Luminous Flora

In the garden, frogs croon,
Dancing daisies laugh at noon.
Beetles buzz in tiny cars,
Their headlights shine like tiny stars.

Butterflies wear silken capes,
Directing traffic, leading shapes.
The roses blush, they can't help it,
While daisies giggle and do a split.

Sunflowers wear their hats quite tall,
While gnomes in glasses stare at all.
They sip on dew from tiny cups,
And share absurdity with the pups.

Oh, what a ruckus, a leafy parade,
Where every bloom has got it made.
They twirl and swirl in colors bright,
In a floral frenzy, pure delight!

Shimmering Pathways in the Wood

In the woods, the squirrels plot,
Over acorns, they form a lot.
A wise old owl rolls his eyes,
At their shenanigans and silly lies.

The trees wear wigs, a funky scene,
While raccoons moonwalk, so obscene.
They giggle at the fallen leaves,
Pretending they are autumn thieves.

A hedgehog dons a tiny crown,
Proclaims himself the prince of town.
While beetles play their tiny drums,
Creating tunes the forest hums.

Yet in this party, spirits thrive,
Nature's dance makes all alive.
With every chuckle, every cheer,
Life's a joke, so let's persevere!

Nature's Celestial Mosaic

In the sky, the clouds collide,
Whimsical shapes they try to hide.
A dragon wearing shades so cool,
Befriends a cow that jumps in pools.

The daisies play a game of tag,
While frogs in helmets start to brag.
Each leaf's a canvas, colors splash,
As laughter echoes, making a crash.

A snail in sneakers, oh so proud,
Sprints ahead, avoiding the crowd.
"Slow is smooth, and smooth is fast!"
He trails behind, but has a blast.

And all around, the merriment flows,
Where nature's secrets, everyone knows.
In this whimsical, vibrant spree,
Every creature laughs, wild and free!

When the Grove Exudes Radiance

In the grove, the laughter spreads,
Where silly songs fill up their heads.
Underneath a tree so wide,
A band of mushrooms starts a ride.

The fireflies twinkle in a race,
While raccoons tumble, losing pace.
Grasshoppers plot their dance routine,
While crickets chuckle, keen and mean.

A rabbit sports a tiny tie,
And hops about, oh me, oh my!
With every jump, he claims the stage,
And earns his stripes at every age.

So let's toast with acorn juice,
And toast to nature's funny noose.
In this grove, where giggles grow,
Every moment's a glorious show!

The Illuminated Arbor

In the forest where squirrels dance,
A light bulb swings in a merry prance.
Raccoons wear shades, oh what a sight,
As fireflies laugh in their glowing flight.

Trees are gossiping with a chuckling breeze,
While branches tickle bees and tease.
A sign on a stump reads, "No more gloom!"
Nature's laughter fills every room.

Underneath the canopy's twinkling lights,
Frogs croak jokes about heights and flights.
Woodpeckers drum a tune just right,
Hosting a party deep into the night.

With roots that wiggle and leaves that grin,
Every critter here is ready to spin.
When day fades into a jovial night,
This arboreal show is pure delight.

Luminality in the Woods

In a glade where giggles bloom,
Sunbeams bounce, dispelling gloom.
Mushrooms wear hats, quite absurd,
As critters gather, sharing a word.

Frolicsome shadows leap and twine,
Squirrels are dressed in suits so fine.
With acorns served on a silver plate,
Every gathering's sure to be great.

Bunnies recount tales loud and clear,
While owls just moan, 'Let's drink some beer!'
Nature's banquet, a hilarious sight,
As laughter erupts like stars at night.

Under the giggling glow so bright,
Creatures exchange wisecracks with delight.
In this glen, where fun is the score,
Every joy is shared, and spirits soar.

Serene Glow of Summer's Bounty

Bees in shades sip on sweet tea,
While ladybugs dance, quite carefree.
Grasshoppers leap with comic flair,
As daisies wave without a care.

The sunbeams play peek-a-boo,
Tickling flowers with sparkles anew.
In this garden, jokes bloom and grow,
As everyone joins in the show.

Critters compete for best clown face,
While butterflies twirl in a racy chase.
Nature's bounty brings laughter near,
As fruit bats play percussion, oh dear!

Under the glow of the summer's light,
The woods are bursting with sheer delight.
With every chuckle woven in air,
Life in the garden is nothing but fair.

The Veil of Glistening Leaves

Leaves are shimmering in green and gold,
Beneath the canopy, stories unfold.
Woodland critters crafting dreams,
While frogs play chess, or so it seems!

The sun spills laughter like sparkling wine,
As chipmunks wear capes, feeling divine.
In the gleam of the evening light,
Nature's jesters are ready to bite.

Squirrels share secrets with trees standing tall,
While mushrooms giggle and beckon us all.
In this magical realm of fun and flair,
Every moment turns into a dare.

As the wind whispers whimsical tales,
The air is thick with laughter prevails.
With a twinkling wink from the moon above,
This woodland party spills over with love.

Twilight's Emerald Embrace

In twilight's glow, the leaves all sway,
They whisper secrets, come what may.
A squirrel dances in the trees,
With acorns tucked beneath its knees.

The shadows stretch, the night takes flight,
Bugs host a rave, oh what a sight!
Branches do the limbo, quite absurd,
As if they're trying to speak a word.

The moonlight winks; she's in on it,
A giggling gnome completes the skit.
Fungi cheer, they've found their groove,
With every twirl, the forest moves.

So join the fun in this leafy patch,
You might just spot a funny match!
In nature's glimmer, endlessly bright,
The silliness reigns through the night.

Leafy Luminaries

Amongst the leaves, the laughter grows,
Tickled by breezes, and no one knows.
A hedgehog jokes with a witty flair,
While fireflies twinkle without a care.

Each branch a stage, for critters bizarre,
A raccoon wearing a shiny car.
Squirrels play chess with acorn crowns,
As owls hoot out their silly sounds.

Under the stars, they throw a feast,
Where mushrooms dance, not the very least!
A ladybug serves up tiny drinks,
While everyone giggles and winks.

With all the joy in nature's hall,
Don't miss the fun; come one, come all!
For in these woods, you'll find delight,
In every shadow, in every light.

Spheres of Glowing Color

Colors swirl in a swirling spree,
As if the rainbows jumped from the sea.
Little sprites toss confetti high,
While tulips blush as they pass by.

Each garden pot has a dancing plan,
With flowers prancing, oh what a clan!
Bees wear hats made of pollen fluff,
Bumping into each other, it's all quite rough.

The bumblebees buzz, and giggles unfold,
Even the daisies refuse to be bold.
They sway to the rhythm of unseen tunes,
Under a sky of glowing moons.

So if you wander where colors collide,
Join the fiesta, let joy be your guide!
For sharing laughter with petals and light,
Makes every moment feel purely bright.

The Light Within the Canopy

The canopy's jokes are simply grand,
As shadows shift with a simple hand.
Branches sway, taking their cue,
From the sunbeam's wink, oh how they flew!

The chirps and hoots, a playful debate,
As the frogs croak out their jesting fate.
A spider spins tales, sticky and neat,
While a raccoon juggles with nimble feet.

The laughter bounces on every breeze,
As leaves wave like they're tickled with ease.
A firefly puts on a show so bright,
Turning the darkness into pure light.

So come, step lightly in this green maze,
Where nature plays tricks and joy stays.
For in every flutter, a giggle is found,
In the leafy laughter all around.

Secrets Under the Shining Canopy

Among the branches, squirrels chat,
With acorns hidden, just like that.
They gossip loud, they play, they tease,
As jaybirds squawk and dance with ease.

A raccoon lurks, he wants a snack,
But can't quite figure out the pack.
He tries to steal a slice of pie,
But only gets a blueberry spry.

In shadows deep, a rabbit grins,
With carrot dreams, he plots and spins.
He hops along in furry delight,
Chasing daylight, oh what a sight!

Under leaves, the laughter rings,
Of creatures plotting fun-filled things.
In this bright place where jokes take flight,
Nature's comedy shines so bright!

Embrace of the Glimmering Trees

A wise old owl with glasses perched,
Reads the news and feels quite searched.
He hoots a pun about the breeze,
With feathered friends who laugh with ease.

The chipmunks juggle acorns' weight,
A circus act, oh how they sate!
With tiny hats and tails that twirl,
The forest wraps them in a swirl.

A fox in boots strolls by with flair,
He tells a tale of chef with care.
Cooking soup with mushrooms grand,
He serves it up by leafy strand.

In the embrace where silliness thrives,
Each critter dreams, each spirit jives.
Beneath the shimmer of bright green leave,
They dance through life, and we believe!

Evergreen Elysium

The pine trees sway in breezy dance,
With pinecone hats, they take a chance.
They hold a ball for birds and bees,
Their feathery tails flutter with ease.

A porcupine dressed up so fine,
Walks with swagger, feeling divine.
He twirls around, a prickly sight,
Dancing under the silver light.

Two frogs debate on jumping high,
"One leap above the clouds," says shy.
The other laughs, "You're out of luck,
I'll just relax here in the muck."

Amid the greens, the giggles blend,
As nature hosts a joyous trend.
In this Elysium where smiles bloom,
The world is bright, there's more than room!

Radiance Among the Roots

In tangled roots, 'neath beams of gold,
A party forms, with tales retold.
The gnomes play cards, the elves make bets,
While snails are slow with no regrets.

A hedgehog spins a yarn so wild,
About a cat who dreamed, a child.
He thought he'd fly upon a kite,
But only soared to reach a fright!

The mushrooms talk of fancy hats,
While fireflies buzz like chatty chats.
They twinkle here, they sparkle bright,
Creating joy through every night.

Among the roots where laughter blooms,
And giggles ring like sweet perfumes.
This radiant place, a funny dream,
Where every creature gleams and beams!

Echoes of Verdant Splendor

In the woods where squirrels prance,
A tree whispered, 'Take a chance!'
But branches laughed, oh what a tease,
While birds showed off their fancy knees.

The mushrooms danced, they've got some flair,
With polka dots, in sunny air.
Leaves chattered secrets, oh so sly,
While ants in tuxedos rolled on by.

Wings of Dawn Amongst the Foliage

A butterfly threw a morning party,
With cupcakes made from dandelion hearty.
The bees all buzzed, in suits so neat,
Saying, 'Join us for honey, it's quite a treat!'

A crow arrived, with a hat so grand,
Sipping dew drops, while making plans.
'Let's dance,' he croaked, 'with flowers in tow!'
And laughter echoed, as they stole the show.

Unveiling Nature's Glow

The sun peeked out from behind a tree,
And said, 'Look at me, bright as can be!'
While clouds in disguise played hide and seek,
Tickling flowers who giggled and squeaked.

Frogs bounced in boots, on lily pads high,
Singing their tunes, oh me, oh my!
The river replied, with a splash and a wink,
'Nature's a show, let's all raise a drink!'

Sylvan Symphony

In a concert hall made of twisted vine,
The crickets chirped, feeling just fine.
With owls as conductors, they took their stand,
While raccoons played drums, in a marching band.

The breeze hummed sweetly, a gentle tune,
As flowers swayed, beneath the moon.
While squirrels on violins played with delight,
A symphony of laughter filled the night.

Luminous Whisperings from Above

In the garden, the veggies chatter,
The carrots gossip, oh what a patter.
Tomatoes grin, in a juicy row,
While radishes laugh, putting on their show.

The sunbeams giggle, skipping on leaves,
Telling tall tales that nobody believes.
A cabbage claims, with a leafy sigh,
That once it danced, and reached for the sky.

Daisies break into fits, oh so bright,
Saying, 'Why not wear your roots overnight?'
A sunflower winks, with petals all aglow,
'Join the fun, it's a party, you know!'

Cucumbers roll with a silly guffaw,
Each inch of soil holds secrets that draw.
Garden gnomes chuckle, hidden in greens,
Sharing funny stories, as silly as dreams.

The Sparkle of Leafy Reverie.

Under the shade, the critters all meet,
A squirrel in a tux, showing off his feet.
The pigeons are pitching jokes from the stone,
While the hedgehogs laugh, they're never alone.

Leaves shimmy and shake, in a breeze so keen,
As chipmunks recount tales of the unseen.
A butterfly flutters, with colors so bold,
Claiming it's the season for stories untold.

Twinkling fireflies buzz around with flair,
Singing sweet songs in the evening air.
A wise old oak, with a creaky, proud grin,
Says, "Join in my shade, let the fun begin!"

Roses tell secrets of love's gentle art,
While violets giggle; they're always so smart.
In the silence, the blooms burst into cheer,
Weaving laughter and joy, all season near.

Whispers of Sunlit Branches

Amid the branches, the chirps collide,
A parakeet jests, with a cockatoo's pride.
They're planning a heist for the feed at noon,
Hiding their schemes like a grinning raccoon.

The flowers are nodding, their petals in sync,
'The bees have a secret, I swear on this pink!'
A daisy named Dot shares a thought so absurd,
'What if we sprout legs and fly like a bird?'

Caterpillars giggle, all snug in the shade,
Dreaming of wings, oh what a parade!
They practice their dance on a soft, mossy floor,
For a garden performance that's never a bore.

With each flicker of light, the jokes fly around,
A woodpecker laughing, a marvelous sound.
Nature's own stand-up, in sunshine's embrace,
Every leaf has a punchline, filled with such grace.

Blossoms of Celestial Dreams

In a meadow bright, where the daisies sway,
A dragonfly swings in its jazzy ballet.
The tulips declare, with a whimsical twist,
'We're the stars of the show, you simply can't miss!'

Atop a tall stem, a grasshopper sings,
Joking 'bout the day and the joy that it brings.
A butterfly joins with a dance and a spin,
While lazy old frogs just chuckle within.

The clouds in the sky, they're puffed up with pride,
They trade gentle jabs, with the sun as their guide.
'We're puffy and fluffy, can't you see the gleam?'
A rabbit hops close, saying, 'What a sweet dream!'

Blossoms of laughter, with pollen so bright,
Filling the air with stories of light.
Each petal, a canvas of joyful delight,
In this garden of wonders, everything's right.

Secrets of the Glistening Grove

In the grove where giggles sprout,
The trees tell jokes, no doubt.
A squirrel with a tiny hat,
Whispers secrets in the chat.

The mushrooms dance in misty glee,
They think they're stars on a spree.
Frogs leap high with laughter loud,
As crickets play to the crowd.

Branches sway with playful cheer,
Revealing tales for all to hear.
A raccoon in shades struts his stuff,
Says life is great, and that's enough!

With every rustle, laughter spreads,
A whimsical world where joy treads.
Nature's jesters take the stage,
In this lively, leafy page.

Enchanted Leaves in the Wind

Leaves twirl round in a silly dance,
As breezes giggle, given a chance.
A caterpillar tries to spin,
But trips and lands with a goofy grin.

The flowers watch with open eyes,
As petals flap like clumsy pies.
A flutter-by in shades of blue,
Tries to tango but misses too.

The wind whispers a playful rhyme,
As creatures chat in sunny clime.
A rabbit hops in oversized shoes,
He claims it's just the latest news.

With every gust, the laughter flows,
Like tickles danced on wiggly toes.
Nature's charm is full of fun,
In the leaf-filled games they run.

The Artisan's Green Brush

An artist tunes his leafy hues,
With laughter painted in the views.
His brush is made of twinkling vines,
Creating giggles with swishing lines.

He splatters joy on every bough,
With flecks of fun that take a bow.
A canvas spread beneath the sun,
Where every stroke is playful fun.

Bees in aprons buzz about,
Fashioning dreams without a doubt.
While snails carry paintbrushes too,
In their slow race, they'll make it through!

With each swirl, the forest sings,
As joy erupts from clever things.
In this artful wild refrain,
Laughter grows like flowers' gain.

Glistening Canopy of Daybreak

Morning peeks with a cheeky grin,
As sunlight tickles every skin.
The branches yawn, stretch wide awake,
And giggle softly; oh, let's bake!

The dew drops laugh, so sparkly bright,
As squirrels perform their acrobatic flight.
A singing bird steals spotlight's fame,
Leaving us all to play the game.

Every rustle is a chuckle shared,
In this canopy, no hearts are scared.
A caterpillar pens a silly song,
Says being small isn't that wrong!

With day's embrace, we all rejoice,
In nature's thread, we find our voice.
So here's to laughter, light, and cheer,
In the glistening grove, let's hold dear!

Illuminated Arches of Nature

In the forest, lights flicker bright,
Squirrels in hats, oh what a sight!
Dancing shadows, a merry parade,
Nature's own circus, unafraid.

Leaves in a twist, like a dancer's turn,
The sun plays tricks, lessons to learn.
Mushrooms grin with polka-dot flair,
While raccoons giggle without a care.

A rabbit with shades and a wild mustache,
Bunny hop parties, they make quite the splash!
Wise old owl snorts with laughter, you see,
While clumsy deer trip over a tree.

Nature's a joker, with laughter and cheer,
In this arc of delight, we gather near.
Join the fun, let worries subside,
Under these arches, let joy be our guide.

Emerald Threads of Light

Woven in green, a zany delight,
Fireflies twirl in the softening night.
A snail on a skateboard, who would have guessed?
An acorn in shades, now that's dressed!

The grass sings songs of the silliest tunes,
While frogs play drums under big, smiling moons.
Mice skate past in their tiny ballet,
As butterflies giggle and float, then sway.

Squirrels in suits strike a suave pose,
As laughter erupts from beneath leafy bows.
They tell of tall tales, too wild to believe,
In this patch of joy, it's hard not to cleave.

Emerald threads weave a tapestry bold,
With quirks that shimmer in stories retold.
Join in the fun, let mischief ignite,
In this merry dance under threads of light.

Vibrant Veils of Serendipity

Under a cloak of vibrant surprise,
A frog wears a crown as he juggles with fries.
The trees chuckle softly, leaves flutter and sway,
As light-hearted critters come out to play.

A wise old turtle dons flashy attire,
While chatty chipmunks spark up a choir.
Bees buzz a tune, oh, what a glee,
As the grasshoppers hop like they're on a spree.

Each twist in the path sparks giggles anew,
With dancing sunbeams that tickle and coo.
A bunny with balloons leads a merry march,
While the clouds join in, softening the arch.

In veils of delight, we twirl and we spin,
The laughter of nature, where silliness wins.
So let's join this fest, with hearts open wide,
In this whimsical world, let joy be your guide!

A Tapestry of Sunlit Fronds

In a sunlit realm, where silliness reigns,
Fronds wave at strangers, exchanging their names.
A chicken in sunglasses struts like a pro,
While the worms stage a dance, putting on quite a show.

Lollipop-colored flowers nod with delight,
As butterflies swirl, painting hues in flight.
The breeze tickles cheeks, laughter echoes clear,
As the ants march in lines, with snacks brought near.

A fox in a jacket, oh what a charmer,
Tell me, my friend, do you feel the glamour?
They sip maple syrup from mystical cups,
While the owls tell tales, as the firefly ups.

Oh, a tapestry bright, woven with glee,
In this garden of laughs, come share in the spree.
So gather your friends, let the fun take its hold,
In this sunny adventure, let memories unfold.

Radiant Canopy

Up in the trees, where squirrels play,
A disco party starts every day.
With acorn hats and nuts in hand,
They dance to beats at nature's band.

Leaves whisper gossip, their secrets loud,
While branches sway, feeling quite proud.
A parrot croons, "Let's take a chance!"
And all the critters join in the dance!

Sunlight spills like lemonade,
Bouncing off leaves that never fade.
The sunbeams laugh, the shadows cheer,
What a hilarious atmosphere!

So lift your gaze, and don't be shy,
There's a raucous show in the sky.
Join the fun, let your spirit soar,
Nature's stage needs just one more!

The Dance of Shimmering Leaves

In the grove where the fun never ends,
Leaves do the cha-cha, making new friends.
A twig taps its feet, joining the beat,
As worms in top hats sway to the heat.

Dandelions wiggle, with fluff in their hair,
While a snail in a shell kicks it without care.
The sun grins down, casting glittery light,
Nature's own party, oh what a sight!

Grasshoppers leap with their fancy moves,
While a lazy old toad just watches and grooves.
The sky lets out chuckles, bright as can be,
Who knew that plants could dance so freely?

So if you wander and hear laughter flow,
Know that the leaves have stolen the show.
Join the ballet of shiny, green flair,
A whimsical world awaits you out there!

Glimmers in the Forest

In the glade where the snickers nest,
Flickering lights put humor to the test.
Fireflies train to be comedians bold,
With jokes so bright, they shine like gold.

"Why did the tree go to school?" it quips,
"To improve its roots and practice its tips!"
With laughter ringing through the thick air,
Every rustle hints at a pun somewhere.

Mushrooms gather, round and proud,
Telling tales just beneath the cloud.
Their cap tips flop, a sight to see,
In this merry wood where the giggles flee.

So next time you hike and feel quite lost,
Remember the trees will cheer at your cost.
Join the hilarity that nature shares,
Among glimmers and giggles, without any cares!

Luminous Tendrils

Glowing vines hang low, a pathway of glee,
Where critters stop by for tea with a plea.
"Pass that jar of sunshine, my friend,
Let's toast to the fun that never must end!"

A raccoon in guise offers up some treats,
While rabbits join in with their tap dance beats.
Laughter erupts from mushrooms so bright,
As fireflies flicker, oh what a sight!

Branches sway gently, to the rhythm they hum,
While ants form a line, marching, "Here we come!"
Clouds overhead giggle, drifting so spry,
Beneath the grand show of the twinkling sky.

So come, take a stroll down that glowing lane,
Where joy is the currency, happiness the gain.
Let the luminous tendrils lead you there,
To a world so ridiculous, you'll stop and stare!

Mosaic of Light and Leaf

In the park, a cat's on a spree,
Chasing shadows, as wild as can be.
Leaves whisper secrets in the breeze,
While squirrels plot mischief with ease.

Sunlight dances on the ground,
A patchwork quilt that spins around.
With every step, a giggle escapes,
From tiny feet in mismatched capes.

Nature's canvas, a sight to behold,
With colors lively and stories untold.
As I trip on roots with laughter most loud,
I'm just a jester among nature's crowd.

So here I twirl, a child once more,
Among the light, I laugh and explore.
The universe chuckles, I reckon so,
In this vibrant space where joy tends to grow.

The Velvet Veil of Nature's Light

Under the canopy, a raccoon in sight,
Stealing my sandwich, what a delight!
Nature's buffet, it seems, never ends,
With critters as thieves, and trees as friends.

Butterflies flutter like clowns with flair,
Juggling nectar without a care.
I tip my hat to the ants on parade,
In tiny tuxedos, their plans never fade.

A squirrel scampers, with acorns to stash,
His little prankster, oh what a splash!
I laugh as he fumbles, a true goofy show,
In this velvet realm, where chuckles flow.

We dance in the light, lost in our fun,
With blooms all around, our laughter is spun.
So here's to the day, and the joys that might creep,
In nature's embrace, we laugh and we leap.

Branches Glinting with Gold

Every leaf a coin, a treasure you'd see,
Shimmering bright, just as happy as me.
A crow starts cawing, oh what a sound,
As if he's declaring I'm royalty crowned!

The sun plays tricks, it's all quite absurd,
Painting the leaves with a magical word.
As I skip and trip, I hear nature's jest,
It giggles along, can't put it to rest.

There's a light breeze that wraps me in cheer,
Tickling my ears as the critters draw near.
With a puff of my cheeks, I blow at a sprite,
Who dances away, oh what a delight!

So let's waltz through this shimmering maze,
Where nature concocts its elaborate plays.
With each step I take, it's laughter I earn,
In this golden grove, I twirl and I turn.

An Odyssey of Glowing Green

In a forested realm, I wander and run,
Chasing moonbeams, oh isn't this fun?
With a giggle from trees, they rustle and sway,
Telling tall tales as they dance in play.

A deer pops out with a look of surprise,
As I mimic stripes like a zebra in disguise.
We share a good laugh, oh what a fine scene,
In this wacky ballet, where all is serene.

The frogs croak a tune, a raucous delight,
As fireflies twinkle, bringing stars to the night.
I join in the chorus, off-key but bold,
In this glowing green tale, I feel ten years old.

So let's raise our voices, a whimsical cheer,
In nature's embrace, there's no room for fear.
Together we frolic, wild and carefree,
In this magical glade, just you and me.

Radiant Branches in Twilight

In the evening glow, the leaves take a bow,
Squirrels in tuxedos dance, what a show!
With acorns galore, they swirl and they twirl,
Making quite the fuss, oh what a whirl!

The winds whisper secrets, the branches just laugh,
A raccoon in a hat, is this nature's own craft?
As shadows play tricks, the owls hoot a tune,
While fireflies flicker, like stars gone too soon!

A mouse in a cape, zooms by on a stream,
While frogs hold a vote, for best evening dream!
The moon takes a peek and snickers a bit,
As nature's own circus begins to commit!

So come join the party, it's wild and it's free,
In this twilight jungle, there's glee, can't you see?
With radiant branches, the night's just begun,
Under the twinkling sky, we all laugh and run!

A Dance of Glistening Petals

Petals on parade, what a glorious sight,
Daisies and sunflowers twirl with delight!
A butterfly slips, and lands on the vine,
Grumbling, 'Not my fault!' it reclaims its shine.

Ladybugs waltz, with their polka-dot suits,
While ants form a band, strumming tiny flutes.
A bumblebee buzz makes them shuffle around,
'No stingers, no drama!' becomes the night's sound.

In the garden so bright, flowers tell jokes,
With petals a-flutter, they poke fun at folks.
When frogs join the fun, with their croaky charm,
Everyone giggles; there's no cause for alarm!

A dance through the night, they play hide and seek,
With the moon chuckling softly, it's all rather bleak.
For when morning breaks, this party will cease,
But we'll dream of the petals, and hope for more peace!

Celestial Canopy of Dreams

Stars above giggle, in a luminous spree,
Casting wishes in whispers, like shadows of glee.
A comet zips past, on a rocket made of cheese,
While planets hold hands, swaying gently in breeze.

Clouds dress in pajamas, oh what a sight!
While moonbeams play peek-a-boo, all through the night.

A spaceship runs late, with aliens in tow,
Exchanging high fives as if they're in a show.

Galactic confetti rains down from afar,
While comets shout, "Aim for that giant space bar!"
The Milky Way whirls with laughter and cheer,
As dreams dance in stardust, they twinkle so near.

So sail through the stars, on a dreamy delight,
With giggles and snickers, we'll take flight tonight.
In this cosmic caper, what wonders we'll find,
In the celestial dreams that tickle our mind!

Glimmers in the Forest's Embrace

In the heart of the woods, where the sunlight sneaks,
The trees wear green gowns, with ruffles and peaks.
A rabbit with glasses reads tales on a log,
While the critters all whisper, "What's next in this fog?"

The brook sings a tune, with a splash and a glint,
As frogs in rare top hats comment on the hint.
Each ripple has gossip, each bubble a tale,
With raccoons debating, 'Is that fish or a snail?'

Squirrels throw acorns, like cheerleaders' gifts,
Playing toss with the nearsighted crow who just drifts.
A chipmunk directs, with a stick as his wand,
As the critters unite, building castles on pond!

So join in the fun, where the magic is true,
With giggles and glimmers, and wonder in view.
In this forest of laughter, let your heart race,
For each twist and turn is pure joy to embrace!

Secrets of the Shimmering Glade

In the woods, the squirrels conspire,
Trading nuts for gossip, they never tire.
Whispers among leaves, secrets unfold,
Who's eating the mushrooms? Oh, do be bold!

Dancing shadows on the ground,
A rabbit joins in, leaping around.
The wise old owl rolls his eyes,
While a critter in disguise, tries to surprise!

They chuckle and chortle, it's quite the scene,
Chipmunks with capes acting so keen.
The trees giggle softly, sharing their tales,
Of the silly mishaps along leafy trails!

Fungi partake in the daily jest,
Whispering tales that none would guess.
In this glade where laughter resides,
Nature's comedy show, where fun abides!

Pictures in the Sun-Dappled Shade

Sunlight streaks through the leafy quilt,
Creating portraits, with shadows built.
A deer poses, trying to look cool,
While a fox sneezes, oh, how rude!

The painterly light dances on ferns,
As bees buzz around, taking their turns.
With petals as palettes, hues do collide,
Even grumpy old hedgehogs can't hide!

Squirrels snap selfies while perched on a log,
But photobombs happen, courtesy of a dog.
There's laughter in every bright, sunny frame,
Nature's a movie; we're all in the game!

A kaleidoscope of antics all day,
In the shade of the trees where we laugh and play.
Memories captured, wild and free,
In this gallery of glee, just you and me!

A Gallery of Green Flecks

In the forest, dots of green play tricks,
Colorful critters perform their antics.
With twigs for paintbrushes, they scurry about,
Creating a masterpiece, there's never a doubt!

A snail in a shell spins art in the dirt,
While a frog on a lily pads gives a flirt.
Each creature a critic, each branch a stage,
Nature's own theater, perfect for any age!

The butterflies flutter, a lively review,
They judge each performance, with wings that ensue.
The rabbits applaud with a hop and a cheer,
In this gallery, laughter is all you hear!

So come take a peek, at the wild and the wacky,
Where Rusty the raccoon gets a tad bit quacky.
In this playful display, joy reigns supreme,
A celebration of nature, a whimsical dream!

Mosaics of Light in Nature's Canopy

Under the canopy, sunbeams cascade,
In patches of laughter, the forest is laid.
Beneath the green ceiling, shadows play pranks,
While raccoons giggle in their mischievous ranks!

A butterfly flutters, lost in its glee,
While a hedgehog rolls past, as sly as can be.
They're creating a ruckus, a homegrown delight,
Mischief unfurling in pure sunlight!

The chitchat of trees whispers words to the sky,
As a squirrel inadvertantly teaches a fly.
With laughs in the air and spirits set free,
Nature showcases its grand comedy!

So leap through the shadows, get lost in the glow,
Where the light plays tricks, and laughter will flow.
A mosaic of moments, both silly and bright,
In this enchanting forest, where joy takes flight!

Shadows of Enchanted Woods

Amidst the trees, the shadows play,
A squirrel tells jokes in a cheeky way.
With leaves as his audience, he can't stop,
Even the owls laugh, wishing to swap.

The branches do dance with a quirky flair,
While chipmunks giggle without a care.
A moth with a mustache joins the cheer,
In this funny land where all creatures steer.

In the corner, a bumpkin snail tells tales,
Of a grand race won by two lazy snails.
The trees lean in with ears wide and keen,
To hear the slapstick in this leafy scene.

A hedgehog in spectacles reads with a sigh,
Words rolling like doughnuts, oh my, oh my!
Each pun that he cracks has the forest aglow,
In this enchanted wood where laughter must flow.

Glorious Arboreal Secrets

In the limbs of the trees, a parrot does sing,
While monkeys throw berries like they're the king.
A giggle erupts from a wise old crow,
As he witnesses chaos, stealing the show.

The flowers gossip of who wore what hue,
With petals a-flutter, they add to the view.
Each breeze brings a tickle, nature complies,
With laughter exploding from roots to the skies.

A squirrel in socks and a top hat so fine,
Recites all the jokes, oh, the grand design!
While rabbits in bow ties applaud the routine,
In this glorious realm, all pranksters convene.

While shadows might slink with a hint of deceit,
These trees stand as guardians, joyful and sweet.
Secrets exchanged with a wink and a wink,
In this arboreal land where giggles don't sink.

Starlit Veins of Green

Underneath the stars, the leaves softly glow,
The owls trade quips, putting on quite a show.
A raccoon in pajamas juggles some fruit,
Laughing at moments that tie in pursuit.

Fireflies flicker, a dance just for fun,
Winking at critters, their night just begun.
A badger in spectacles counts the stars bright,
Misplacing his numbers, he ends with a fright.

The grass whispers secrets, then bursts into glee,
As frogs on a log croak in harmony.
A turtle named Larry, with flair and some zest,
Has a joke about speed; oh, he loves to jest!

As the moon holds its breath, the laughter soars high,
In starlit veins where the clever hearts lie.
Each giggle creates a bright constellation,
In this green, twinkling space of elation.

A Tapestry of Light

With sunbeams entwined, they weave a grand tale,
Of rabbits wearing dresses who bravely set sail.
A hedgehog with flair serves tea to a fox,
Amidst a backdrop of shimmering clocks.

The bees start a band, buzzing tunes in the glade,
While butterflies dance in their colorful parade.
They twirl and they spin, in the warm, golden rays,
Creating a spectacle that brightens the days.

A turkey in shades starts a disco so wild,
With disco balls swinging, he dances like a child.
The trees form a circle, encouraging fun,
As the sunsets roll out, setting laughter on the run.

In this tapestry woven of humor and light,
The jungle's alive, a delightfully sight!
Every creature is laughing, in rhythm and rhyme,
In this vibrant scene, they all share their time.

Luminescent Petals in the Twilight

In the garden, flowers gleam,
They dance and giggle like a dream.
Petals shimmer in the night,
Chasing moonbeams, oh what a sight!

Bees wear tiny sunglasses bright,
Buzzing jokes, oh what delight.
They pollinate with comic flair,
Creating laughs in fragrant air.

The daisies trade their silly tales,
While violets share their wind-powered gales.
With every breeze, they're throwing shade,
In this blooming circus, joy is made.

At dusk, the petals start to sway,
In laughter's arms, they twirl and play.
As stars peek out, they wink and sprout,
A floral comedy, never in doubt!

Chasing Dappled Light

Sunbeams tickle leaves above,
As squirrels make a laugh-filled shove.
Chasing shadows, they prance and hop,
In this game, they never stop.

A rabbit wears a top hat bold,
As grasshoppers spin tales of old.
Every flicker makes them smile,
In this dappled space, they linger awhile.

The breeze carries a jolly tune,
While daisies dance beneath the moon.
Each light that dips, a joyful chase,
In nature's playground, laughter's grace.

As twilight draws the curtain tight,
The woodland comes alive with light.
Chasing hues and giggles' sound,
In every corner, fun is found!

Nature's Illuminated Tapestry

Woven threads of giggles bloom,
In every nook, they chase the gloom.
Sunlit patches, a tapestry bright,
Where owls crack jokes in the soft twilight.

Butterflies wear polka-dot capes,
Leading the fun with silly shapes.
Nature's canvas, adorned with glee,
A symphony of whimsy and spree.

The trees whisper secrets, oh so sly,
As dandelions puff clouds in the sky.
Each sprout a jester, ready to jest,
In this kingdom, laughter's the guest.

With starlit threads, the night adorns,
As blooms giggle 'til the morns.
A radiant show where colors blend,
In nature's kindness, joy transcends!

The Soft Hand of Radiance

A gentle light with a cheeky wink,
Tickles the night, makes shadows think.
Frogs in bow ties croak a tune,
As fireflies dance like little loons.

The grass giggles underfoot,
While crickets give a loud salute.
Each glowing spark, a friend in flight,
Guiding through the giggly night.

Under the moon, the world's gone mad,
Every flower showcases what it had.
Swaying softly, they can't keep still,
In this game of joy, they feel the thrill.

The stars humor with a twinkling cheer,
Guiding the laughter, drawing near.
In this soft hand, they play and prance,
Where every shimmer leads to a dance!

Shadows That Glow

Underneath the glowing moon,
A raccoon tried to sing a tune.
He tripped over roots, a clumsy show,
Swaying like a star in daft tableau.

Squirrels chattered, wearing hats,
Debating loudly over acorn stats.
A rabbit in a tux joined the fray,
Throwing confetti in a silly way.

The owls hooted like a jazz band,
Dancing to music none could understand.
Trees bobbed along, swinging with glee,
As shadows whispered, "Join the spree!"

But just when the fun hit a peak,
The raccoon sneezed—oh, what a cheek!
Leaves flew up, like a party pop,
And all around, their laughter wouldn't stop.

The Beaming Canopy

Sunbeams tickled the laughing leaves,
For dancing trees and playful thieves.
A squirrel juggled nuts without a care,
While a crow squawked, shouting, "Look, I'm rare!"

The laughter echoed, ringing clear,
As ants formed lines for a train of cheer.
"Next stop, the picnic!" shouted a bee,
Buzzing wild, not quite so free.

Vegetable pals joined the move,
Tomatoes danced, trying to groove.
Carrots twirled, so sprightly and bright,
While cucumbers laughed at their lost flight.

The sun began to set, soft and slow,
Filling the forest with a golden glow.
The trees all sighed in a funny way,
As the critters promised to meet each day.

Where the Green Light Flickers

A firefly held a sign up high,
"Dance with me, don't be shy!"
While the frogs croaked their loudest beat,
Tapping toes in the warm, green heat.

A hedgehog rolled in starry night,
Wobbling around, what a funny sight.
He bumped the mushrooms, they all giggled loud,
Creating a pillowy, bouncing crowd.

Ferns flailed wildly in the green scene,
Whirling like they're part of some cuisine.
"Is this the dance we call the jig?"
Asked a mushroom in a ruddy wig.

The night wrapped up with a goofy cheer,
As friends proclaimed, "We love it here!"
The flickers danced in the moonlit sky,
With laughter echoing, oh my, oh my!

Twilight Among the Trees

Twilight draped the forest snug,
With critters cozy, sharing a hug.
A raccoon, dapper, with a bowtie bright,
Claimed he'd out-dance the stars tonight.

The trees swayed lightly to a breeze,
While squirrels held tail races with ease.
A fox shared jokes, oh what a prank,
Making even the oldest tree crank!

Toadstools bubbled, giggling near,
Spinning tales, spreading good cheer.
Lightning bugs lit up with flair,
A nighttime gala, free of despair.

As the moon peeked through the leafy veil,
The laughter soared, it did not fail.
"Let's keep it up till first light beams!"
They cheered and spun in their wildest dreams.

Dance of the Radiant Foliage

In the woods, leaves do a jig,
They trip and swirl, quite big a gig.
Squirrels join in, they laugh and play,
With acorn hats, they're bright and gay.

The sunbeam winks, a cheeky cheer,
The branches sway, full of good cheer.
Hopping to tunes of rustling breeze,
Nature's band plays with such great ease.

Watch the flowers bust a move,
Petals swirl with a dazzling groove.
Stems twirling, what a sight to see,
A botanical party, joyous and free!

So join the dance, do not delay,
In this leafy club, let's sway away.
With every step, let laughter burst,
For nature's humor, we surely thirst.

Enchanted Gardens of Light

In a garden where gnomes do chat,
They argue over who's the fanciest hat.
Sunflowers peek, too tall to hide,
While daisies giggle with petals wide.

Butterflies flutter, oh what a chase,
Dodging raindrops in a merry race.
Ladybugs laugh, their shells aglow,
Painting polka dots in the rows below.

A toad croaks jokes, oh what a fool,
Making frogs leap into a cool pool.
Chasing ripples and splashes loud,
A comedy show for the critter crowd!

With twinkling lights strung on each vine,
The plants put on a show, oh so fine.
Under the moon, they twirl with glee,
In this fairytale place, wild and free!

Nature Speaks in Shimmers

When fireflies chat, they flicker and glow,
With secret whispers only they know.
Grasshoppers hop, with a comic grace,
Stumbling and tumbling in the open space.

A wise old owl, perched up high,
Winks at the moon and gives a sigh.
"Whooo" he hoots, then snickers a bit,
As a hedgehog rolls by, not one bit fit!

The brook sings songs, all bubbly and bright,
With fish caught giggling, a slippery sight.
They splash around, minds full of cheer,
Dancing through droplets, year after year.

Nature laughs, in colors and sound,
Joyful whispers all around.
So lend an ear, let's shade this strife,
In nature's humor, we find our life.

The Luminance of Twining Vines

In a tangle of vines, a raccoon derides,
His tangled tail, oh how it slides!
Laughter erupts from flowers nearby,
As the critter fumbles, oh my, oh my!

A twirling vine grumbles, "Cut it out, mate!"
While the tulips giggle, "A sorry fate!"
A dandelion puffs, all soft and round,
"Let me give you a lift, let's roll on the ground!"

A snail in a shell, he's slowing the scene,
With sticky trails glistening and green.
He chuckles softly, "I may be slow,
But in this crazy race, I steal the show!"

So twine with joy, let's giggle and spin,
In the garden of laughter, we'll all Win!
Join hands with the wild, in this fancy design,
In a world of whimsy, where the sun always shines.

Echoes of Luminous Bloom

In the garden, laughter grows,
Petunias gossip, who knows?
Sunflowers dance in silly hats,
Winking at the chubby cats.

Bees buzz tunes of pure delight,
Chasing pollen, taking flight.
While daisies crack a goofy grin,
Their petals flapping in the wind.

A cucumber plays the jester's role,
Telling jokes that make you roll.
The carrots giggle, snicker, shout,
As the spinach pouts and twirls about.

Amidst this flora, all is bright,
With nature's punchline, what a sight!
Bouncing flowers, what a crew,
Setting the stage for this funny hue.

Glowing Fragments of Life

In the twilight, fireflies blink,
With tiny jokes, they poke and wink.
A moth with glasses reads the stars,
While crickets strum on rusty bars.

Underneath the twilight sky,
Nonsense reigns, oh my, oh my!
With all the giggles in the air,
Life glows bright without a care.

A frog recites its latest tune,
Complaining 'bout the fickle moon.
While frogs and flutes in harmony,
Ribbit, ribbit, quite comically!

Every plant has something fun,
With roots that tickle in the sun.
For life's a dance, a quirky play,
With glowing bits to make our day.

The Light that Wears a Crown

A glowing orb, oh what a sight,
Declares itself the king of night.
With crown of stars and sparkly cheer,
It tickles shadows, brings them near.

The moon's a joker, full of jive,
Splashing silver, keeping alive.
A comet zooms, his tail a cape,
Creating laughs, a cosmic shape.

Each planet hums a silly song,
While asteroids dance along so wrong.
The light that wears a crown, divine,
Is just a prankster on cloud nine.

So when you gaze up, don't forget,
The universe is a funny set.
Bright laughter beams across the night,
With every twinkle, pure delight.

Dappled Dreams in Sundrenched Groves

In sunny groves, the shadows play,
Chasing butterflies all day.
The trees gossip like old friends,
Sharing tales that never ends.

A squirrel slips, a comic fall,
As acorns giggle, "Not at all!"
A parrot squawks, it's quite absurd,
Telling secrets without a word.

Dappled light, it winks and beams,
Tickling the ground, like children's dreams.
Every flutter, every shake,
Is proof the forest loves to bake!

So dance among the dappled rays,
Let laughter spark your sunny days.
In forests where the funny thrives,
You'll find the joy that truly jives.

www.ingramcontent.com/pod-product-compliance
Lightning Source LLC
Chambersburg PA
CBHW070751220426
43209CB00083B/447